INTERPLAY

with Angels

Richard Kusiolek

To order additional copies of this book, contact:
Xlibris
844-714-8691
www.Xlibris.com
Orders@Xlibris.com

ISBN: 979-8-3694-0842-1 (sc)
ISBN: 979-8-3694-0841-4 (e)

Print information available on the last page

Rev. date: 10/03/2023

Contents

Interplay

I gather streams that flow through my pen to make patterns for my view –
Elusive, glancing back at me are faces from Eternity –
Some I have known, will know again – while, some, perhaps are just Fate's whim –
Attendant companies that stray enchanted here, their interplay –

A teasing glimpse, a jesters' ploy to show this world is just a toy –
With-in, beyond, the universe uncounted
Entities traverse

God's Well

The sun, Gods well, where people draw
the gold that seals the light that heals –
Returning ever and again to sip anew –
it's golden rim overflowing on the earth
in endless cycles of re-birth –

– Where people dredge reflected treasure
that, flowing cold, in veins of gold
(secure within Earth's mantle-folds,)
have warmed again where water runs
over the scattered sands of the sun.

All the reflections of the sun,
(sunlit pleasures, golden treasures)
add to the thirst you felt before –
Forever would you ask for more –
Till the night folds around the Bright one
and from the sands, no gold is won.

Thirsting children, in the darkness,
The chalice hidden in the night
Seek the endless morning
in the light that God extends us.
Accept the draught that's proffered
in the very cup it's offered –
Nor seek from the Provider's hand
a larger vessel or degree
other than is given free –

3

Freedom

Through empty halls, the people search
austere buildings – the hallways merge
where silent echoes whisper at doors
of chambered men sent from both shores.

With urgent tones the poor entreat –
In learned tomes the sages treat
with august theories the human plight –
While in the rim of Freedom's light
powerful men with large domains
lobby and strain for personal gain.

Within these walls people's choices
heed or ignore the people's voices –
Besieged, beleaguered, they
now implore us –
"How may we answer such a chorus?"

If brave Freedom's
torch-light flutters
In smoke-filled rooms,
and by the gutters,
the same light glows majestically –
in quiet homes and industry
that seek their gain – but no one injures,
for these shed light upon their brother.

A Month of Sundays

Stop for a moment, dear friend of mine,
Quietly talking, and sharing some time
will lighten the day, and take some of the load
from your mind, your eyes say is feeling the goad
of clocks, and flocks of problems you're fielding
in the time that you're seeing as so very
unyielding –

So, stop for a moment – in
the day's foment –
How much is gained when
your mind is so strained
by scheduled reminders in Black
Leather Binders?

Stay for a little the pace
you are setting
by the clock's face – your
own you are letting
be furled and frowning –
without any clowning,
how can your day be worth any pay?

If my wish for you were answered –
All the tired thoughts are transferred
to the first day of the week.
For thirty days the sentence passed for
working without the rest of the fun days
and enforce a month of Sundays!

Mediumship and its Development

Mediumship is a sharing of time and space in your mind and soul without giving up either – True mediumship takes nothing away, but adds to the one that shares.

No one is brought to the point of channeling with the lack of a teacher, but at all points, the student can refuse to continue, and may elect to do so without censure – All is free will, and what is not done in one space but can be done in another. The choice is all-inclusive, and leaves no path unavailable to the seeker.

Take your trial of a new path when you feel the need and guidance to do so. Try and let the way be natural. No way is too difficult, but may seem so at the time, and if you cannot let go of the difficulty in your mind, try to do so in your spirit, blessing it, and letting it go.

Now, the way clears, and you can be led – more than that your teacher will not do.

When these criteria are met, you are sent no more than you can handle, and are given those messages and teachings as are readily understandable to you or those for whom you are channeling. These are to be given to the seeker without change or interpretation, as the analytical mind has no place in this matter, but, instead, follows the leading of the spirit. Always trust to spirit for truth, and keep the message pure.

Pride of Mind

The lions of my mind are sinewy beasts –
They move with grace born of strength.
The group as though integral – yet, none
observe the others as they pace –

And, so, myself move, in pride of mind –
as though together in space only,
not joining yet, not in touch,
but whole, complete in themselves.

No communication exists in them –
They are Alone in their strengths.
What common peril or prey brings their
combined attention?
A roar might be heard – but why roar
at nothing – and there is nothing –
No sound – Nothing occurs,
but the shifting of these, and they
wait –

God's son and heir, when in great need,
may enter in that Golden Lair –
His passage safe, his stride is sure,
and matches that of the
mighty pride.
For fear would
never enter here –
But welcomed is the loving heir.

Orbits

I spent a universe with you last night –
and left this world behind
Out in the tormenting stillness of Light
into the Realms of mind –

We came together both of us –
we learned together, both of us –
Separate, we found that Space
was entry to another's place
which, quite unlike intended,
left wounds that have not been mended.

Untimely was the convergence
of our two worlds – Opponents,
defensive, on the invaded ground,
could not perceive the pathway round
that sets aside their lonely pride
with orbits that would not collide.

I spent a universe with you last night
and saw those worlds as two –
Wheeling thru Spirals
of Echoing Light
Each is central, to their view.

We came together, both of us –
We learned together, both of us –
Together, we found that Space
was a mirror to each other's face.
Released by the offended –
the wounds have all been mended.

Lose your limits

Lose your limits, cease to cower
before this immensity yourself empower.

Above the Light is Darkness –
Below is endless Space
All between is Energy fully to be used
to create, to form, to shape;
Again to dissipate

Finite, Infinite –
Ever-existing Absolutes
Expressing All that Is.
Above is not, Below is not;
Confusion enters in –
Till viewed aright, in
Space of Light
Upon the Brow of Heaven.

Point of View

How can I build foundations
for my 'Castle in the Air' –
when a touch upon the surface
of that Whirling Dervish there –
would tear apart the corners
of my castle that I share
with cloud images around me,
their forms so fine and rare,
transient as rainbows
above the Earthen sphere.
They would dissipate forever –
At the Shadow's touch interred –
as a myriad drops of water,
as frozen chrystals in its lair;
That brought into the Sun's light,
flashback rainbows in the Air.

The Veil of Tomorrow

I won't promise 'forever'
never my heart
could offer this bondage
"Till death do us part"

"Till the point of departure,"
This is my vow –
My loving is given
Completely for now.

I will search not to know
What in the future lies
For the Veil of Tomorrow
Is shading my eyes.

But how do I love thee,
Now my hand holds.
This moment in freedom
Our Present Enfold.

The Singer and The Song

Beloved the Singer, by Whose Song
the universe was sung –
Sacred the Name, Whose cadence
is found in everyone –
We ask that Thy council
and Wish the path we tread –
Beside Thy Living Waters
receive Thy truth as bread.
Remove the Shackles of Silence
that we, too, may release
All those we held in malice
with words of love and peace.
Restrain us from entering
attachments once again.
The Kingdom Thine,
Its Power & Song
Throughout the Ages reigns.

Telephone Song

Hello, my dear, so glad to hear– Yes,
I missed you too –
The hours are so few! .. Sometimes
soon... No, this afternoon
is all tied up, appointments just lined up!
As soon as I can - we really must plan.
I'm not sure – I don't know –
I really must go!
So glad that you rang up –
Slowly I hang up.
We talk round-about, so casually, without
making it plain – chatting in vain.
The phone is a buffer, it would
be so much rougher
meeting your eyes –
Without telling lies
How can I stop this?
For I cannot miss - the
doubt that I'm feeling
about my revealing
My need to be free –
Yet I want to be
with you as a friend.
The hours that we spend
in a union of mind
are the best of their kind.
If I told you now –
Would you stay anyhow?
If on His occasion –
without evasion, I'd made this confession,
would my profession
of friendship's caring
be worth your sharing?
Goodbye, my dear – So nice to hear.

Angels - A Vision

The brilliant tones of passion
at heart must be subdued
on the Palette of Love the colors
all are softly-hued.

The voices of Love are even tender,
with words and music that will render

Soft the sounds, and gentle the lyrics
So important
with Love's Atmospherics

Parrot Song

I found a parrot in my soul
Perched unseen, he was in control –
I watched that parrot start to preen,
recite his song, the words between –
money, money needs money, money

What a parrot song was this!
'cause the words were all amiss.
There in my heart, and my head
the refrain of the parrot said – refrain

But now I have my money's-worth
choose to use – there is no dearth
Send happy songs into the air
and find money everywhere! refrain

Money in my heart – to spend
on good times, to give, or lend
Money in my mind-to use
what to buy, or sell, or choose
Money in my Soul – un-tolled
Never was a mint so cold!

So, now I have my moneys-worth
choose to use, there is no dearth
Send happy songs into the air –
you'll find money every
where! Refrain

Fire Garden

Come enter Winters' door with me
and watch the Salamanders play
in golden light, from the fire-side bright
where the flickering sprites are beaming.

They seek out homes where folk reside
that love to dream by the fire-side
and wander the dancing garden
with a mind entranced by gazing
at fire-flowers in the blazing
and bright images in coals

These spirits graced the light of Spring
with gentle dews of dawning
These same had glanced
thru Summer's sun
and flamed with crisp
Autumn's leaves –
then gathered close to Winter's door
to wait beside the fire.

The garnered dreams that there abide
the gleeful spirits of the fire hide
in the depths of the Fire Garden
You can seek your
dreams within its maze
delve the Golden Oracle's blaze
before it turns to ashes

Come enter Winter's door with me –
and watch the Salamanders play
in golden light, by the fire-side bright
where the flickering sprites are beaming.

Going Home

At times the sound of Heaven's voice, stilled and chilled by the soul's own choices,
made in doubt of the chosen route; now at the end of another dead-end –
sends out a cry "Tell me why, so much pain for so little gain"
Comes back a voice, still and small, "never was there pain at all.

And, now, within, I hear the call, "Return, return,
and enter in among old friends left on this side
of the curtain stretching far out of sight
Allow the memories so dim, gathering dust, but burning
within, to send a light into the night, that sets it all afire.

The sons are returning – and the children are learning
The worlds now sensing its ultimate cleansing.
Going Home, rewards appear – Going Home,
amend all fear
Going Home, the time is near, – Going Home,
fresh songs you hear.

Again, within, I hear the call, "Return, return, and
enter in among old friends, you left this side of the curtain
stretching far out of sight.
Allowing the memories so dim, gathering strength,
and burning with-in –
To form a line into the night, setting all afire–

Rimming and brimming the edges alight
of clouds encircling the darkness in flight
Dimmed in the Luminance coming in sight –
they're filling and spilling with torrenting might
Changing, arranging, and setting the right
all turbulence felt in quiet delight.

Return – Return

Take heart – it is not further away than your acceptance
– not beyond your sight or hearing – closer than your
dreams – and sooner than you believe.

The Passage of the Lost Watch

The 'Time of Day' sees hours flow
that count the intent of mind and soul;
In ordered sequence passing by
the guarded barriers we never try

Note the Time it seems to be,
– not the time you hold; set free,
Cradled in Space,
mid future and past,
Negating both,
and blended so that Now begins;
A glimpse is seen
thru the Hallway – and out.

And now, aware, unshackled, free;
Captive no more, the prison flees.

The channels of Time
make way for you.
The currents of Space
envelope you.
The Passage of the
Lost Watch enter
Search the Universe at its center

Acknowledge the being that you are
Star-flung offspring from afar

The Crystal Gazer

The Lady in Winter was standing alone
She held in her hand a glittering stone
She heard her own voice in sorrow declare –
"Who stands beside me, tomorrow to share?"

She was lovely and cold, this Lady of Old.
Her fires were blue, but the center was gold.
She watches in crystal, she sees her own face,
Beside it, another, within the stones' space.

The thawing of Winter, tomorrow is seen –
In the heart of the crystal, the golden light gleams –
The blue of the fires of the azure blue skies,
Reflect the content in the Lady's glad eyes.

Wings

With a Flutter of wings,
Then silent respect, the awesome
Brilliance of dawn.
Hazy outlines of
Trees remain moments before
Darkness envelops all.
The once-stately tree
Bends in charred humiliation

Fantasy

Freeing one's mind.
So that one might indulge.
In a small dose
Of fantasy
Which, undoubtedly, Will be
Abruptly halted by
The glaring eyes of the Rising sun
The Wind caresses.
The earth, gently parting leaves
A single tree shivers.

Leaving

When the time came
For you to leave
I began frantically.
Searching my mind
For something,
anything,
I could ask you.
Just so I could
To be with you
A moment longer.

While you faded
Into the darkness
I stood.
Straining my eyes
Trying to memorize
Wishing you would turn.
Around
And yet knowing.
How embarrassed I would be.
If you caught me staring.
I hated myself.
For not having called
To you.
I wanted to tell you.
Again, and again
How wonderful
I felt When I was with you.

Ode to Womanly Perfection

Oh! Fools, are we?
Can you not be a myth to me?
Why do I go on so to feel but only to die?
Truth dies on this vine.
Suffering slowly destroys my immortal soul.

Forget this, for an island such as yours can never be bridged.
The waves sweep it aside.
To fight but not to gain, I push onward to new shores.
I shall stand but alone for the grave is my only home.

The footprints in the sand shall disappear.
Slow the crumbling sand takes away all trace.
I bid you farewell for I have played the game.
Not even a thorn-burdened crown shall be mine
I walk away in disgrace.

Oh! callous and wicked fops they be!
Who swallows pride to rush upon the sea.
To clutch only droplets
Of diluted sleep

Richard Theodor Kusiolek was an early visionary of space-related technologies in Northern California's Silicon Valley. In Gage Park High School and Lyons Township College, Richard studied Graphic Arts and enjoyed sketching with ink. After Graduate School at San Francisco State University, he began a successful career in Marketing and Advertising. Kusiolek was a faculty adjunct professor at the University of Phoenix and had been a contributing author for Via Satellite Magazine, UK Satellite Evolution Asia, APSCC, and China Communications (CIC). His fiction novels were, "Angels in the Silicon, Man of Seven Shadows, and "Wake County 9 am." His earlier published poems were "Star Traveling- Inspirational Stars" and "Deborah Moon."

Printed in the United States
by Baker & Taylor Publisher Services